MW01296390

MARTIN LUTHER'S SMALL CATECHISM

Table of Contents

The Ten Commandments:

The Simple Way a Father Should Present Them to
His Household

The First Commandment

You must not have other gods.

What does this mean?

We must fear, love, and trust God more than anything else.

The Second Commandment

You must not misuse your God's name.

What does this mean?

We must fear and love God, so that we will not use
His name to curse, swear, cast a spell, lie or deceive,
but will use it to call upon Him, pray to Him, praise Him
and thank Him in all times of trouble.

The Third Commandment

You must keep the Sabbath holy.

What does this mean?

We must fear and love God, so that we will not look down on preaching or God's Word, but consider it holy, listen to it willingly, and learn it.

The Fourth Commandment

You must honor your father and mother. [So that things will go well for you and you will live long on earth].

What does this mean?

We must fear and love God, so that we will neither look down on our parents or superiors nor irritate them, but will honor them, serve them, obey them, love them and value them.

The Fifth Commandment

You must not kill.

What does this mean?
We must fear and love God, so that we will neither harm nor hurt our neighbor's body, but help him and care for him when he is ill.

The Sixth Commandment

You must not commit adultery.

What does this mean?

We must fear and love God, so that our words and actions will be clean and decent and so that everyone will love and honor their spouses.

The Seventh Commandment

You must not steal.

What does this mean?

We must fear and love God, so that we will neither take our neighbor's money or property, nor acquire it by fraud or by selling him poorly made products, but will help him improve and protect his property and career.

The Eighth Commandment

You must not tell lies about your neighbor.

What does this mean?

We must fear and love God, so that we will not deceive by lying, betraying, slandering or ruining our neighbor's reputation, but will defend him, say good things about him, and see the best side of everything he does.

The Ninth Commandment

You must not desire your neighbor's house.

What does this mean?

We must fear and love God, so that we will not attempt to trick our neighbor out of his inheritance or house, take it by pretending to have a right to it, etc. but help him to keep & improve it.

The Tenth Commandment

You must not desire your neighbor's wife, servant, maid, animals or anything that belongs to him.

What does this mean?

We must fear and love God, so that we will not release his cattle, take his employees from him or seduce his wife, but urge they to stay and do what they ought to do.

The Conclusion to the Commandments

What does God say to us about all these commandments?

This is what He says:

``I am the Lord Your God. I am a jealous God. I plague the grandchildren and great-grandchildren of those who hate me with their ancestor's sin. But I make whole those who love me for a thousand generations."

What does it mean?

God threatens to punish everyone who breaks these commandments. We should be afraid of His anger because of this and not violate such commandments. But He promises grace and all good things to those who keep such commandments. Because of this, we, too, should love Him, trust Him, and willingly do what His commandments require.

Part II: The Creed

The Creed: The Simple Way a Father Should Present it to His Household

The First Article: Creation

I believe in God the Almighty Father, Creator of Heaven and Earth.

What does this mean?

A. I believe that God created me, along with all creatures. He gave to me: body and soul, eyes, ears and all the other parts of my body, my mind and all my senses and preserves them as well. He gives me clothing and shoes, food and drink, house and land, wife and children, fields, animals and all I own. Every day He abundantly provides everything I need to nourish this body and life. He protects me against all danger, shields and defends me from all evil. He does all this because of His pure, fatherly and divine goodness and His mercy, not because I've earned it or deserved it. For all of this, I must thank Him, praise Him, serve Him and obey Him. Yes, this is true!

The Second Article: On Redemption

And in Jesus Christ, His only Son, our Lord, Who was conceived by the Holy Spirit, born of the Virgin Mary, suffered under Pontius Pilate, was crucified, died and was buried, descended to Hell, on the third day rose again from the dead, ascended to Heaven and sat down at the right hand of God the Almighty Father. From there He will come to judge the living and the dead.

What does this mean?

I believe that Jesus Christ is truly God, born of the Father in eternity and also truly man, born of the Virgin Mary. He is my Lord! He redeemed me, a lost and condemned person, bought and won me from all sins, death and the authority of the Devil. It did not cost Him gold or silver, but His holy, precious blood, His innocent body -- His death! Because of this, I am His very own, will live under Him in His kingdom and serve Him righteously, innocently and blessedly forever, just as He is risen from death, lives and reigns forever. Yes, this is true.

The Third Article: On Becoming Holy

I believe in the Holy Spirit, the holy Christian Church, the community of the saints, the forgiveness of sins, the resurrection of the body, and an everlasting life. Amen.

What does this mean?

I believe that I cannot come to my Lord Jesus Christ by my own intelligence or power. But the Holy Spirit called me by the Gospel, enlightened me with His gifts, made me holy and kept me in the true faith, just as He calls, gathers together, enlightens and makes holy the whole Church on earth and keeps it with Jesus in the one, true faith. In this Church, He generously forgives each day every sin committed by me and by every believer. On the last day, He will raise me and all the dead from the grave. He will give eternal life to me and to all who believe in Christ. Yes, this is true!

Part III: The Lord's Prayer

The Simple Way a Father Should Present it to His Household

The Introduction

Our Father, Who is in Heaven.

What does this mean?

In this introduction, God invites us to believe that He is our real Father and we are His real children, so that we will pray with trust and complete confidence, in the same way beloved children approach their beloved Father with their requests.

The First Request May

Your name be holy.

What does this mean?

Of course, God's name is holy in and of itself, but by this request, we pray that He will make it holy among us, too.

How does this take place?

When God's Word is taught clearly and purely, and when we live holy lives as God's children based upon it. Help us, Heavenly Father, to do this! But anyone who teaches and lives by something other than God's Word defiles God's name among us. Protect us from this, Heavenly Father!

The Second Request

Your Kingdom come.

What does this mean?

Truly God's Kingdom comes by itself, without our prayer. But we pray in this request that it come to us as well.

How does this happen?

When the Heavenly Father gives us His Holy Spirit, so that we believe His holy Word by His grace and live godly lives here in this age and there in eternal life.

The Third Request May

Your will be accomplished, as it is Heaven, so may it be on Earth.

What does this mean?

Truly, God's good and gracious will is accomplished without our prayer. But we pray in this request that is be accomplished among us as well.

How does this happen?

When God destroys and interferes with every evil will and all evil advice, which will not allow God's Kingdom to come, such as the Devil's will, the world's will and will of our bodily desires. It also happens when God strengthens us by faith and by His Word and keeps living by them faithfully until the end of our lives. This is His will, good and full of grace.

The Fourth Request

Give us our daily bread today.

What does this mean?

Truly, God gives daily bread to evil people, even without our prayer. But we pray in this request that He will help us realize this and receive our daily bread with thanksgiving.

What does ``Daily Bread" mean?

Everything that nourishes our body and meets its needs, such as: Food, drink, clothing, shoes, house, yard, fields, cattle, money, possessions, a devout spouse, devout children, devout employees, devout and faithful rulers, good government, good weather, peace, health, discipline, honor, good friends, faithful neighbors and other things like these.

The Fifth Request

And forgive our guilt, as we forgive those guilty   of sinning against us.

What does this mean?

We pray in this request that our Heavenly Father will neither pay attention to our sins nor refuse requests such as these because of our sins and because we are neither worthy nor deserve the things for which we pray. Yet He wants to give them all to us by His grace, because many times each day we sin and truly deserve only punishment. Because God does this, we will, of course, want to forgive from our hearts and willingly do good to those who sin against us.

The Sixth Request

And lead us not into temptation.

What does this mean?

God tempts no one, of course, but we pray in this request that God will protect us and save us, so that the Devil, the world and our bodily desires will neither deceive us nor seduce us into heresy, despair or other serious shame or vice, and so that we will win and be victorious in the end, even if they attack us.

The Seventh Request

But set us free from the Evil One.

What does this mean?

We pray in this request, as a summary, that our Father in Heaven will save us from every kind of evil that threatens body, soul, property and honor. We pray that when at last our final hour has come, He will grant us a blessed death, and, in His grace, bring us to Himself from this valley of tears.

Amen.

Part IV: Holy Baptism

The Sacrament of Holy Baptism: The Simple Way a Father Should Present it to His Household

I.

What is Baptism?

Baptism is not just plain water, but it is water contained within God's command and united with God's Word.

Which Word of God is this?

The one which our Lord Christ spoke in the last chapter of Matthew: ``Go into all the world, teaching all heathen nations, and baptizing them in the name of the Father, the Son and of the Holy Spirit.''

II.

What does Baptism give? What good is it?
It gives the forgiveness of sins, redeems from death and the Devil, gives eternal salvation to all who believe this, just as God's words and promises declare.

What are these words and promises of God? A. Our Lord Christ spoke one of them in the last chapter of Mark: ``Whoever believes and is baptized will be saved; but whoever does not believe will be damned.''

III.

How can water do such great things?

Water doesn't make these things happen, of course. It is God's Word, which is with and in the water. Because, without God's Word, the water is plain water and not baptism. But with God's Word it is a Baptism, a grace-filled water of life, a bath of new birth in the Holy Spirit, as St. Paul said to Titus in the third chapter:

``Through this bath of rebirth and renewal of the Holy Spirit, which He poured out on us abundantly through Jesus Christ, our Savior, that we, justified by the same grace are made heirs according to the hope of eternal life. This is a faithful saying."

IV.

What is the meaning of such a water Baptism?
It means that the old Adam in us should be drowned by daily sorrow and repentance, and die with all sins and evil lusts, and, in turn, a new person daily come forth and rise from death again. He will live forever before God in righteousness and purity.

Where is this written?

St. Paul says to the Romans in chapter six: ``We are buried with Christ through Baptism into death, so that, in the same way Christ is risen from the dead by the glory of the Father, thus also must we walk in a new life."

Part V: Confession

How One Should Teach the Uneducated to Confess

What is confession?

Confession has two parts:

First, a person admits his sin

Second, a person receives absolution or forgiveness from the confessor, as if from God Himself, without doubting it, but believing firmly that his sins are forgiven by God in Heaven through it.

Which sins should people confess?

When speaking to God, we should plead guilty to all sins, even those we don't know about, just as we do in the ``Our Father," but when speaking to the confessor, only the sins we know about, which we know about and feel in our hearts.

Which are these?

Consider here your place in life according to the Ten Commandments. Are you a father? A mother? A son? A daughter? A husband? A wife? A servant? Are you disobedient, unfaithful or lazy? Have you hurt anyone with your words or actions? Have you stolen, neglected your duty, let things go or injured someone?

Part IV: The Sacrament of the Altar

The Simple Way a Father Should Present it to his Household

The Sacrament of the Altar:

What is the Sacrament of the Altar?

It is the true body and blood of our Lord Jesus Christ under bread and wine for us Christians to eat and to drink, established by Christ Himself.

Where is that written?

The holy apostles Matthew, Mark and Luke and St. Paul write this:

``Our Lord Jesus Christ, in the night on which He was betrayed, took bread, gave thanks, broke it, gave it to His disciples and said: ``Take! Eat! This is My body, which is given for you. Do this to remember Me!'' In the same way He also took the cup after supper, gave thanks, gave it to them, and said: ``Take and drink from it, all of you! This cup is the New Testament in my blood, which is shed for you to forgive sins. This do, as often as you drink it, to remember Me!''

What good does this eating and drinking do?

These words tell us: ``Given for you'' and ``Shed for you to forgive sins.'' Namely, that the forgiveness of sins, life and salvation are given to us through these words in the sacrament. Because, where sins are forgiven, there is life and salvation as well.

How can physical eating and drinking do such great things?

Of course, eating and drinking do not do these things. These words, written here, do them: ``given for you'' and ``shed for you to forgive sins.'' These words, along with physical eating and drinking are the important part of the sacrament. Anyone who believes these words has what they say and what they record, namely, the forgiveness of sins.

Who, then, receives such a sacrament in a worthy way?

Of course, fasting and other physical preparations are excellent disciplines for the body. But anyone who believes these words, ``Given for you,'' and ``Shed for you to forgive sins,'' is really worthy and well prepared. But whoever doubts or does not believe these words is not worthy and is unprepared, because the words, ``for you'' demand a heart that fully believes.

Morning Prayer

My Heavenly Father, I thank You, through Jesus Christ, Your beloved Son, that You kept me safe from all evil and danger last night. Save me, I pray, today as well, from every evil and sin, so that all I do and the way that I live will please you. I put myself in your care, body and soul and all that I have. Let Your holy Angels be with me, so that the evil enemy will not gain power Over me. Amen.

Evening Prayer

My Heavenly Father, I thank You, through Jesus Christ, Your beloved Son, that You have protected me, by Your grace. Forgive, I pray, all my sins and the evil I have done. Protect me, by Your grace, tonight. I put myself in your care, body and soul and all that I have. Let Your holy angels be with me, so that the evil enemy will not gain power over me. Amen.

Made in the USA
Las Vegas, NV
13 September 2022

55242866R00016